SABAN'S POWER RANGERS SUPER SAMURAI

HEAD-TO-HEAD

26 POWERFUL MATCHUPS THAT MUST BE SEEN!

BY PAUL BECK

SCHOLASTIC

■SCHOLASTIC
www.scholastic.com

Published by Scholastic Inc., 557 Broadway, New York, NY 10012; Scholastic Canada, LTD. Markham, Ontario

Scholastic and associated logos are trademarks of Scholastic Inc.

becker&mayer!
BOOK PRODUCERS

Produced by becker&mayer!, LLC. 11120 NE 33rd Place, Suite 101, Bellevue, WA 98004 www.beckermayer.com

If you have questions or comments about this product, please visit www.beckermayer.com/customerservice.html and click on the Customer Service Request Form.

Designer: Sam Dawson
Editor: Dana Youlin
Managing editor: Michael del Rosario
Image research: Katie del Rosario and Emily Zach
Production coordinator: Jennifer Marx

Printed, manufactured, and assembled in New Jersey, USA 11/12

10 9 8 7 6 5 4 3 2 1
ISBN: 978-0-545-53857-2

12425

The Samurai Power Rangers face off against their Nighlok enemies in epic battles to defend the world from evil. For each matchup you'll see the skills, stats, and special weapons that each side brings to the contest, so you can decide the winner. You'll also find a summary of the latest Power Rangers shows, along with the experts' picks for the winners in each battle.

THE MATCHUPS

Red Samurai Ranger vs. Deker · · · · · · · · · · · · · · · 8
Pink Samurai Ranger vs. Dayu · · · · · · · · · · · · · · · 10
Green Samurai Ranger vs. Rofer · · · · · · · · · · · · · · · 12
Blue and Pink Samurai Rangers vs. Doubletone · · · · · · · · 14
Samurai Battlewing vs. Desperaino · · · · · · · · · · · · · · 16
Green Samurai Ranger vs. Moogers · · · · · · · · · · · · · · 18
ApeZord vs. Antberry · 20
Yellow Samurai Ranger vs. Negatron · · · · · · · · · · · · · 22
Green and Blue Samurai Rangers vs. Spitfangs · · · · · · · · 24
LionZord vs. Tooya · 26
Battlewing Megazord vs. Robtish · · · · · · · · · · · · · · · 28
Bull Megazord vs. Maldan · · · · · · · · · · · · · · · · · · 34
Super Blue Samurai Ranger vs. Armadeevil · · · · · · · · · · 36
TurtleZord vs. Duplicator · · · · · · · · · · · · · · · · · · 38
SharkZord vs. Yamiror · 40
Secret Red Samurai Ranger vs. Fiera · · · · · · · · · · · · · 42
Gold Samurai Ranger vs. Octoroo · · · · · · · · · · · · · · · 44
DragonZord vs. Skarf · 46
Claw Battlezord vs. Papyrux · · · · · · · · · · · · · · · · · 48
BearZord vs. Switchbeast · · · · · · · · · · · · · · · · · · 50
Claw Armor Megazord vs. Grinotaur · · · · · · · · · · · · · · 52
Light Megazord vs. Epoxar · · · · · · · · · · · · · · · · · · 54
Samurai Shark Megazord vs. Rhinosnorus · · · · · · · · · · · 56
Claw Armor Megazord and Samurai BattleCannon vs. Dreadhead · · · 58
Claw Battlezord North and Bull Megazord vs. Serrator · · · · 60
Samurai Gigazord vs. Master Xandred · · · · · · · · · · · · · 62

POWER RANGERS SAMURAI

Hundreds of years ago, an army of evil monsters called Nighlok invaded our world through gaps in space and time. After a long battle, Samurai Rangers defeated the Nighlok and forced them into the Netherworld, sealing them in with special Power Symbols. Knowing the seals might someday be broken, the Rangers passed their Power Symbols down to their children, so that new generations of Samurai Rangers could protect the Earth.

The present story begins when evil Master Xandred, Lord of the Nighlok, breaches the surface of the Netherworld's Sanzu River in his ship. Master Xandred has reawakened from his long imprisonment at the river bottom. He begins a new Nighlok assault on our world, sending his minions through the gaps between both worlds to spread havoc and misery. Master Xandred plans to flood the Earth as the waters of the Sanzu River swell with the tears of the "crybaby humans."

The summons goes out to a new team of warriors, teenage descendants of the original Samurai Rangers. Their leader is Jayden, the Red Ranger, who has trained as a Samurai from a young age. The others are Blue Ranger Kevin, Pink Ranger Mia, Green Ranger Mike, and Yellow Ranger Emily. Together the Rangers battle Master Xandred's Nighlok monsters with their Samurai training, Symbol Power over the elements, and their Zords—marvelous machines in animal form that expand into powerful fighting vehicles. The Zords harness the energy of the animals they are associated with—the Lion, the Dragon, the Turtle, the Bear, and the Ape.

In the Netherworld, Master Xandred has a team of his own. Squid-faced Octoroo is his advisor, researching the Nighlok archives for new ways to help Master Xandred carry out his evil plans. Dayu, a human musician who became a Nighlok in a deal to save her husband's life, soothes Master Xandred's constant, terrible headaches with the misery-laden sound of her deformed instrument, the harmonium. From his ship Master Xandred sends a parade of Nighlok monsters, one after another, to attack the human world.

The story follows the Samurai Rangers as they battle invasion after invasion of Master Xandred's Nighlok monsters. Some, like the sword-wielding Robtish, are powerful fighters. Others, like the spirit-eating Splitface, have special powers that must be neutralized before they can be defeated. Every Nighlok must be defeated twice: once in normal form, and again when it reappears in giant MegaMonster mode. The Rangers fight the MegaMonsters from the cockpits of their Zords, which morph into Mega Mode and combine to form giant humanoid fighting machines called Megazords.

As the story continues, the Rangers gain a new teammate in the fisher-man Antonio, the Gold Ranger. He is the childhood friend of Jayden's who has trained as a Samurai on his own. Antonio brings with him the OctoZord in the

form of an octopus. The Rangers also cross paths with Bulk and his nephew Spike, bumbling Samurai wannabes whose attempts at Samurai training always end in comical disaster.

As the Rangers face increasingly powerful Nighlok invaders, they must learn more skills, how to use more powerful weapons, and uncover new Zords. Jayden discovers how to unlock the BeetleZord, and the Rangers win back the captured TigerZord, while Antonio unlocks the power of the lobster-like ClawZord. The powers of the new Zords provide the Rangers with new weapons like the Five Disc Beetle Cannon and the flying Samurai Battlewing.

Weaving through the tale is the mysterious half-human, half-Nighlok Deker. He is cursed to live a twilight life between his two forms until he fights a final duel against the ultimate opponent, the Red Ranger Jayden. Deker is not concerned with Master Xandred's plans. He is single-minded in his pursuit of

the Red Ranger, sometimes even fighting against the Nighlok to save Jayden for himself.

Meanwhile, Octoroo has discovered that the Red Ranger has power over a special Sealing Symbol that can imprison Master Xandred in the Netherworld forever. Now Master Xandred's attacks are aimed not just at the Rangers together, but also at Jayden in particular. At one point a traitorous Nighlok named Arachnitor tries to get Jayden's Sealing Symbol Power for himself. Master Xandred stops the plot just in time and drags Arachnitor back to the Netherworld for punishment.

At the climax of the story, Jayden leaves his Power Discs with Kevin so that the Blue Ranger can lead the team. The Red Ranger goes by himself to face Deker in the ultimate duel. The fight will take every ounce of his skill and training, and only a self-sacrificing move will let him finally defeat Deker.

RED SAMURAI RANGER VS. DEKER

The Red Power Ranger leads the team of Samurai Power Rangers in their fight to defend humankind from the evil Nighlok. Deker, though half Nighlok himself, doesn't take sides in that battle. For Deker, it's personal. He's after the Red Ranger alone, in a quest to match swords with an opponent worthy of his skills.

Red Ranger / Jayden

Jayden, the Red Ranger, began his Samurai training as a small boy. He is the leader of the Power Rangers and a formidable warrior. His skill as a swordsman is unmatched among the members of his team. When powered by his Lion Disc, the Red Ranger's Spin Sword morphs into the gigantic Fire Smasher. His Zord is a lion.

INFO	
Species	Human
Realm	Human world
Weapons	Spin Sword, Fire Smasher
Skills	Power over fire
Special Attack	Blazing Strike

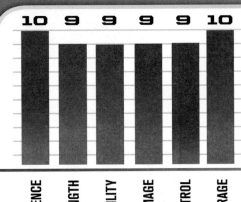

STATS

10	9	9	9	9	10
INTELLIGENCE	STRENGTH	AGILITY	DAMAGE	CONTROL	COURAGE

The Red Power Ranger and Deker are as evenly matched as any human and Nighlok (or half-Nighlok) can be. Deker believes Jayden to be the only enemy worthy of his sword, Urumasa. For his part, the Red Ranger must be in top condition. If Deker senses that Jayden has been weakened in another battle, he will break off the fight, waiting for the ultimate duel when their strengths are even. Their nearly equal fighting skill will make this contest long and hard-fought.

Deker

Half human, half Nighlok, Deker is cursed never to rest until he fights a duel with his ultimate opponent, the Red Ranger. Deker will even step in to fight against the Rangers' Nighlok enemies in order to save the Red Ranger for himself. Deker's half-human nature lets him stay in the human world without returning to the Sanzu River.

STATS

INTELLIGENCE	STRENGTH	AGILITY	DAMAGE	CONTROL	COURAGE
9	10	9	9	10	10

INFO

Half human, half Nighlok	**Species**
Human world and Netherworld	**Realms**
Urumasa sword	**Weapons**
Can morph between human and Nighlok forms	**Skills**
Lightning-fast swordplay	**Special Attack**

PINK SAMURAI RANGER VS. DAYU

Unbeknownst to each other, the Pink Power Ranger and Dayu have something in common: music. Mia is an excellent singer. Dayu's most prized possession is her harmonium, an evil instrument morphed into its twisted shape from the guitar she had in her former human life. But when these two fighters meet in battle, the only music you'll hear is the sound of clashing swords.

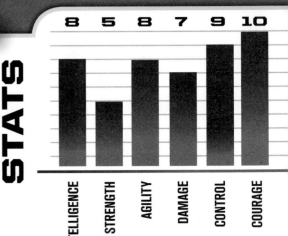

Pink Ranger / Mia

Mia, the Pink Ranger, uses her Sky Fan to command the power of air with devastating results against the Nighlok. Among the Power Rangers she takes the role of a caring big sister. Mia loves to cook, but the dishes she makes for her friends might work better as weapons, if she could only feed them to the Nighlok. Her Zord is a turtle.

INFO

Species	Human
Realm	Human world
Weapons	Spin Sword, Sky Fan
Skills	Power over air
Special Attack	Airway

STATS

	INTELLIGENCE	STRENGTH	AGILITY	DAMAGE	CONTROL	COURAGE
	8	5	8	7	9	10

THE SHOWDOWN

Perceptive and intuitive, the Pink Power Ranger senses that Dayu's anger and hatred of humans are rooted in some deep sadness from the past. That could cause problems if Mia's feelings make her hesitate to attack. Although Dayu would prefer to spend her time playing sorrowful music aboard Master Xandred's ship, she is also a skilled fighter. But the Pink Ranger's Samurai training should make her more than a match for the half-Nighlok troubadour.

Dayu

Born in the human world, the musician Dayu traded away her human existence and entered the Netherworld in a deal with a Nighlok to save the life of her beloved Deker. But the bargain was a trick. Though spared from death, Deker remembers nothing of their former life. Dayu takes out her sorrow and anger on humans with a vengeance.

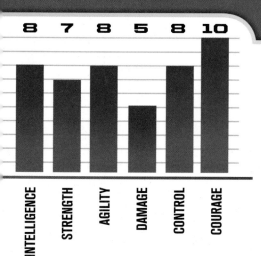

STATS

8	7	8	5	8	10
INTELLIGENCE	STRENGTH	AGILITY	DAMAGE	CONTROL	COURAGE

INFO

Half human, half Nighlok	**Species**
Netherworld	**Realm**
Harmonium	**Weapons**
Fills her music with centuries of human misery	**Skills**
Harmonium conceals a hidden dagger	**Special Attack**

GREEN SAMURAI RANGER VS. ROFER

When Rofer bursts on the scene with flying fists, frightened humans run for cover. That's just what Rofer's master wants. As the humans' fear and misery rises, so do the red waters of the evil Sanzu River. Facing Rofer, the Green Power Ranger brings quick wit and the elemental power of the forest.

Green Ranger / Mike

Mike, the Green Ranger, isn't as serious about training as some of the other Power Rangers. But he makes up for it by being very good at thinking on his feet and coming up with unusual moves in a fight. His Zord is a bear, and he commands the element of forest.

INFO

Species	Human
Realm	Human world
Weapons	Spin Sword, Forest Spear
Skills	Power over forest
Special Attack	Forest Vortex

STATS

INTELLIGENCE	9
STRENGTH	7
AGILITY	8
DAMAGE	9
CONTROL	7
COURAGE	10

THE SHOWDOWN

Rofer's advantage is the sheer punching power of his fists. That, and his ability to stretch his arms over seemingly infinite distances could make this Nighlok a challenge for one Ranger alone to beat. But Rofer is too boastful and not too bright. The Green Power Ranger's strengths are his creativity and inventive fighting style. As long as he watches out for Rofer's Arm Stretch sneak attacks, Mike should be able to hold his own against the two-fisted Nighlok.

Rofer

With giant fists and a somewhat-less-than-giant brain, Rofer isn't the sharpest weapon in Master Xandred's Nighlok arsenal. But he's good at frightening humans and pummeling Power Rangers. Rofer's stretchable arms let him attack from a distance, and he can even send his fists to sneak up on his victims from underground.

STATS

	3	9	8	7	8	9
	INTELLIGENCE	STRENGTH	AGILITY	DAMAGE	CONTROL	COURAGE

INFO

Nighlok	**Species**
Netherworld	**Realm**
Giant fists	**Weapons**
Long-distance pummeling	**Skills**
Arm Stretch	**Special Attack**

13

The Power Rangers are taught by their Mentor Ji that their greatest accomplishments come when they work together as a team. Teamwork is the key when the Blue and Pink Rangers fight the Nighlok Doubletone, whose two-pronged blasts of energy are too much for one Ranger to handle alone.

Blue & Pink Rangers

Kevin, the Blue Ranger, and Mia, the Pink Ranger, team up to bring the elemental powers of water and air together in the fight. With the Blue Ranger's Dragon Disc and Pink Ranger's Turtle Disc, their Spin Swords morph to the powerful Hydro Bow and Sky Fan.

INFO

Species	Human
Realm	Human world
Weapons	Spin Swords, Hydro Bow, Sky Fan
Skills	Power over water and air
Special Attack	Dragon Splash, Airway

STATS

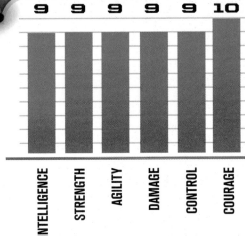

9	9	9	9	9	10
INTELLIGENCE	STRENGTH	AGILITY	DAMAGE	CONTROL	COURAGE

THE SHOWDOWN

The matchup may seem uneven at first, with one Nighlok facing two Power Rangers. But each of Doubletone's Tiger Tidal Wave and Super Tsunami attacks produces a double blast of energy. It takes one Ranger to take on each half. The Blue and Pink Rangers' teamwork will be put to the test. They'll need to use their animal Power Discs to morph their Spin Swords into more powerful elemental weapons if they want to defeat this Nighlok.

Doubletone

This Nighlok con artist brings misery to the world by tricking humans into giving up their dreams. Even other Nighlok think Doubletone is a lowlife. But devious trickery isn't his only weapon. Doubletone is an excellent hand-to-hand fighter, and he can also conjure up deadly double energy blasts.

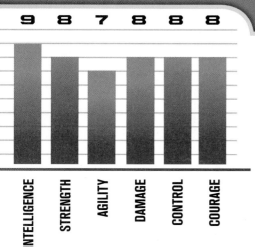

STATS

9	8	7	8	8	8
INTELLIGENCE	STRENGTH	AGILITY	DAMAGE	CONTROL	COURAGE

INFO

Nighlok	**Species**
Netherworld	**Realm**
Energy blasts	**Weapons**
Devious persuasion	**Skills**
Tiger Tidal Wave, Super Tsunami	**Special Attack**

15

SAMURAI BATTLEWING VS. DESPERAINO

When the Power Rangers first defeat a Nighlok, the battle is only half over. The vanquished Nighlok returns in MegaMonster mode, a giant version of its former self. To fight the MegaMonster, the Rangers call on the Mega Mode power of their animal Zords. Battling a flying Nighlok like Desperaino calls for a flying Zord combination: the Samurai Battlewing.

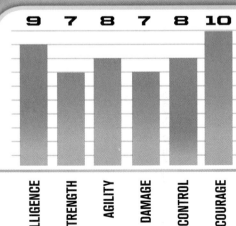

Samurai Battlewing

The Red, Green, and Blue Rangers use Symbol Power to morph the TigerZord, SwordfishZord, and BeetleZord to Mega Mode. Then they unite the three Zords to form the Samurai Battlewing. This airborne Zord can fly with the speed and agility of a fighter jet. The three Rangers pilot the Battlewing together.

INFO

Type	Zord combination
Realm	Human world
Weapons	Blaster
Skills	Flight, Vortex Spin
Special Attack	Charging Slash

STATS
ADJUSTED FOR MEGA SIZE

9	7	8	7	8	10
INTELLIGENCE	STRENGTH	AGILITY	DAMAGE	CONTROL	COURAGE

ZORD SHOWDOWN

Desperaino is sure to take the battle to the air, where he has been undefeated until now. The Red, Green, and Blue Power Rangers will need their best piloting skills to engage the airborne Nighlok in a dogfight. Powerful blasts from Desperaino's spear have the potential to knock the Battlewing out of the sky. The Ranger pilots will try to use the special Vortex Spin maneuver to evade the Nighlok blasts and get in close for a final strike.

Desperaino

The MegaMonster Nighlok Desperaino has the ability to create a rain of despair that drains all hope from his human victims. As their misery rises, so do the evil waters of the Sanzu River. When he unfurls the tentacled, umbrella-like membrane on top of his head, this Nighlok can fly through the air.

8 6 9 7 8 9

INTELLIGENCE STRENGTH AGILITY DAMAGE CONTROL COURAGE

STATS
*ADJUSTED FOR MEGA SIZE

	INFO
Nighlok MegaMonster	**Species**
Netherworld	**Realm**
Energy-blasting spear	**Weapons**
Flight	**Skills**
Rain of Pain	**Special Attack**

GREEN SAMURAI RANGER VS. MOOGERS

With fish-like heads and mouths full of evil-looking teeth, Moogers wriggle between the Netherworld and ours through cracks in time and space. They're sent by Master Xandred to wreak havoc and terrorize humans. To the Power Rangers, Moogers are usually more annoying than dangerous. Things get a little trickier when Moogers attack in large numbers.

Green Ranger / Mike

When he first became the Green Power Ranger, it took Mike a little time to learn that he was better off fighting as a member of a team than on his own. In the words of Mentor Ji, "One Samurai is strong, but a team is unbeatable." That said, a Mooger isn't much of a challenge.

INFO

Species	Human
Realm	Human world
Weapons	Spin Sword, Forest Spear
Skills	Power over forest
Special Attack	Forest Vortex, Leaf Storm

STATS

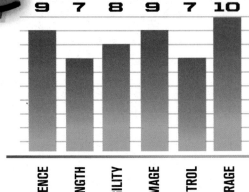

9	7	8	9	7	10
INTELLIGENCE	STRENGTH	AGILITY	DAMAGE	CONTROL	COURAGE

THE SHOWDOWN

For all their scary looks, Moogers are ill-matched against the Samurai training of the Power Rangers. Each Mooger carries only a simple weapon. It's usually a sword, but could be a spear, axe, chain, a laser blaster, or a bow and arrows. The Green Ranger should have no trouble defeating a Mooger in a fight. But given the Moogers' habit of attacking in groups, the Green Ranger may have to repeat the contest over and over again.

Moogers

Moogers are the foot soldiers of the Netherworld. They squirm out of gaps between the worlds to spread panic among humans. Though they look fearsome, a single Mooger is no match for a Power Ranger. But where there's one Mooger, there are usually many others. Master Xandred seems to have an endless supply of them.

STATS

	2	3	5	4	6	8
INTELLIGENCE						
STRENGTH						
AGILITY						
DAMAGE						
CONTROL						
COURAGE						

INFO

Mooger	**Species**
Netherworld	**Realm**
Sword, spear, chain, axe, or arrows	**Weapons**
Mindless mob mayhem	**Skills**
Can appear in giant form	**Special Attack**

APEZORD VS. ANTBERRY

The ApeZord belongs to Emily, the Yellow Power Ranger. The Zord is normally small enough to fit in her hand, but when the Rangers go up against a Nighlok MegaMonster, Emily uses her Symbol Power to morph the ApeZord to giant Mega Mode. This time the opponent is Antberry, a slippery character who blasts his enemies with globs of disgusting Sanzu slime.

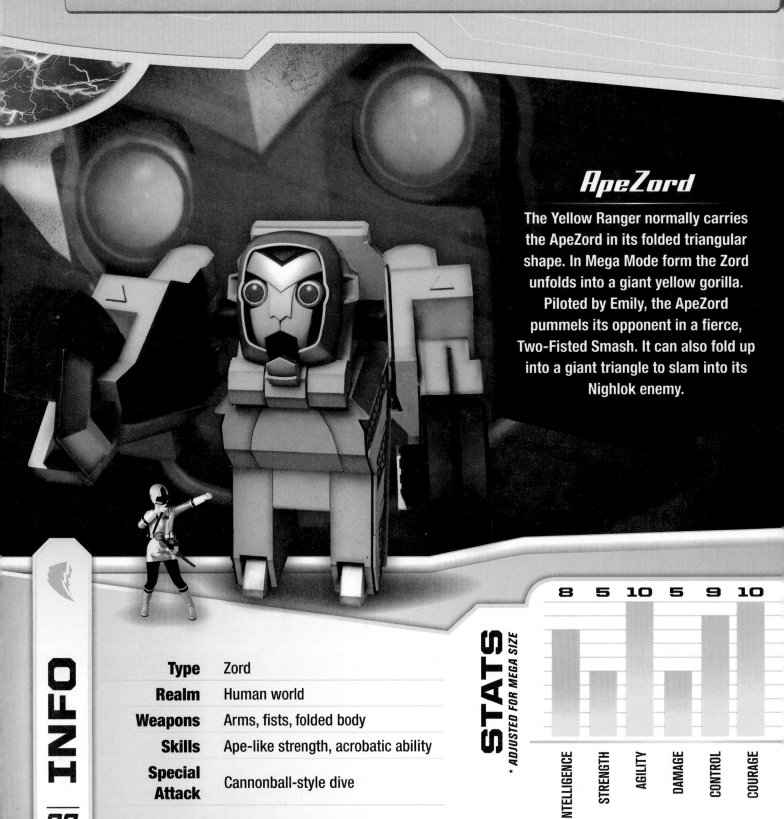

ApeZord

The Yellow Ranger normally carries the ApeZord in its folded triangular shape. In Mega Mode form the Zord unfolds into a giant yellow gorilla. Piloted by Emily, the ApeZord pummels its opponent in a fierce, Two-Fisted Smash. It can also fold up into a giant triangle to slam into its Nighlok enemy.

INFO

Type	Zord
Realm	Human world
Weapons	Arms, fists, folded body
Skills	Ape-like strength, acrobatic ability
Special Attack	Cannonball-style dive

STATS
*ADJUSTED FOR MEGA SIZE

INTELLIGENCE	STRENGTH	AGILITY	DAMAGE	CONTROL	COURAGE
8	5	10	5	9	10

ZORD SHOWDOWN

Antberry will mount a double attack, with slime and saber. If the Yellow Power Ranger can pilot her ApeZord to a high place, above the reach of Antberry's sword, the Zord can fold up and drop like a cannonball on the monster's head. If not, the ApeZord must charge in close, under the saber's swing. The slimy Nighlok will be too slippery to grab, but a barrage of solid punches from the Zord can take him down.

Antberry

Antberry isn't all that bright, but he's hardworking and loyal to his Nighlok master. A coating of slippery slime makes this monster nearly impossible to grab. However, the slime can dull his own weapons. In normal Nighlok form, Antberry wields a stone axe, but in MegaMonster mode he fights with a curved saber.

	3	7	6	7	5	9

INTELLIGENCE · STRENGTH · AGILITY · DAMAGE · CONTROL · COURAGE

STATS
*ADJUSTED FOR MEGA SIZE

Nighlok MegaMonster	**Species**
Netherworld	**Realm**
Slime Shooter, giant saber	**Weapons**
Slimes enemies' weapons, making them slippery	**Skills**
Sanzu Slime	**Special Attack**

INFO

The cruel Nighlok Negatron bursts on the scene, hurling insults at humans. His zingers don't just hurt his victims' feelings, they cause physioal pain. Emily, the Yellow Power Ranger, knows just how they feel. She was teased as a child, but her older sister taught her to ignore hurtful words. In her fight against Negatron, she'll let her Spin Sword and Earth Slicer do the talking.

Yellow Ranger / Emily

Emily, the Yellow Ranger, is the youngest of the Power Rangers. Her older sister was originally destined to become the Yellow Ranger, but when she became seriously ill, Emily stepped in. The Yellow Ranger harnesses the power of the earth. Her Zord is an ape.

INFO

Species	Human
Realm	Human world
Weapons	Spin Sword, Earth Slicer
Skills	Power over earth
Special Attack	Seismic Swing

STATS

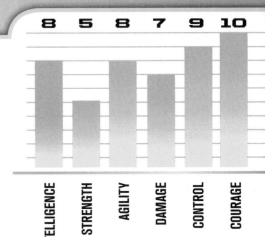

8	5	8	7	9	10
INTELLIGENCE	STRENGTH	AGILITY	DAMAGE	CONTROL	COURAGE

THE SHOWDOWN

Negatron's insults aren't easy to ignore. He has the ability to sense his opponent's innermost doubts and insecurities, then twist a tiny bit of truth into a painful putdown. He will aim his barbs at Emily's desire to live up to the example of her sister. But Emily has trained hard to master her Samurai skills as the Yellow Power Ranger. She has the mental strength to ignore Negatron's insults and use her elemental earth power to defeat him.

Negatron

Known as the Prince of the Putdown, Negatron needs no weapons other than his sharp, insulting tongue. This Nighlok's insults inflict both mental and physical harm. For added damage, Negatron can zap his opponent with a blast of energy from the three eyes on the back of his head.

STATS

7	7	5	6	7	9
INTELLIGENCE	STRENGTH	AGILITY	DAMAGE	CONTROL	COURAGE

INFO

Nighlok	**Species**
Netherworld	**Realm**
Insults and putdowns	**Weapons**
Uses insults to cause physical pain	**Skills**
Three-eyed Zapazoid	**Special Attack**

When Spitfangs appear, mayhem is sure to follow. These Netherworld monsters open their reptilian mouths impossibly wide, then spew fireballs at anything that gets in their way. Spitfangs travel in pairs, so it takes a pair of Rangers to even up the fight. The Green and Blue Power Rangers have just the right combination of inventiveness and skills to handle them.

Green & Blue Rangers

Mike, the Green Ranger, is creative in his approach to fighting, but he is sometimes not as serious about training as he could be. Kevin, the Blue Ranger, is diligent about training but sometimes needs to lighten up a bit. Together, with Mike's creativity and Kevin's martial-arts mastery, they make a formidable team.

INFO

Species	Human
Realm	Human world
Weapons	Spin Swords, Forest Spear, Hydro Bow
Skills	Power over forest and water
Special Attack	Forest Vortex, Dragon Splash, Double Slash

24

STATS

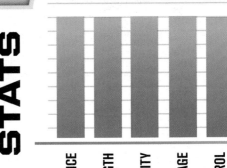

9	9	9	9	9	10
INTELLIGENCE	STRENGTH	AGILITY	DAMAGE	CONTROL	COURAGE

THE SHOWDOWN

The Spitfangs have only one fighting mode, but it's a tough one to beat. With a double barrage of fireballs coming at them, the Green and Blue Power Rangers will have a difficult time getting close enough to the monsters for normal swordwork. Even combining the power of their Spin Swords for a double slash may not do the trick. The Rangers' best bet will be to attack the Spitfangs with the power of the Forest Sword and Hydro Bow.

Spitfangs

A Spitfang is mostly head, with a pair of legs for getting around and a tail behind for balance. The head looks like a cross between an alligator and a snake, with a bit of dragon thrown in for good measure. Like Moogers, they are found in both regular and giant MegaMonster size.

STATS

2	7	2	7	5	8
INTELLIGENCE	STRENGTH	AGILITY	DAMAGE	CONTROL	COURAGE

INFO

Spitfang	**Species**
Netherworld	**Realm**
Fireballs	**Weapons**
Fireball spitting	**Skills**
Even more fireballs	**Special Attack**

LIONZORD VS. TOOYA

When a defeated Nighlok returns in MegaMonster form, it's time for the Power Rangers to morph their animal Folding Zords into Mega Mode fighting machines. The Red Power Ranger leads the charge at the helm of the mighty LionZord. In this contest, the LionZord goes up against Tooya, one of Master Xandred's first minions to be sent to terrorize the human world.

LionZord

In its small form, the LionZord likes to scamper up to perch on Jayden's shoulder or sit purring in the palm of his hand. But when the Zord morphs into Mega Mode, it transforms into a ferocious, roaring lion. In the cockpit, the Red Ranger controls the LionZord with his Mega Blade wielding a Furious Lion Howl and Strong Striking Skills.

INFO	
Type	Zord
Realm	Human world
Weapons	Furious Lion Howl
Skills	Blazing speed, Strong Striking Skills
Special Attack	Pentagonal Fury

STATS
* ADJUSTED FOR MEGA SIZE

9	6	9	6	9	10
INTELLIGENCE	STRENGTH	AGILITY	DAMAGE	CONTROL	COURAGE

Tooya will mount a strong attack, blasting away at the LionZord with bolts of energy from both of his swords. The LionZord will have to get in close for a counterattack, but Jayden must steer clear of the Nighlok's armor skirt, where gnashing teeth could trap and immobilize the Zord. The Red Power Ranger will have his strongest attack with the Pentagonal Fury strike, where the LionZord folds up and flies straight into the enemy, blazing with flames.

Tooya

This Nighlok earns the nickname "Skirtface" from the leering eyes and mouth on the lower part of his armor. Tooya first slipped out of a crack between the worlds at the head of an army of Moogers. In MegaMonster mode, he slashes right and left with a sword in each hand.

5	5	6	6	5	9
INTELLIGENCE	STRENGTH	AGILITY	DAMAGE	CONTROL	COURAGE

STATS
* ADJUSTED FOR MEGA SIZE

Nighlok MegaMonster	**Species**
Netherworld	**Realm**
Pair of short swords	**Weapons**
Mouth in skirt can grab and hold Zord	**Skills**
Laser blasts	**Special Attack**

INFO

27

BATTLEWING MEGAZORD VS. ROBTISH

To fight the Nighlok Robtish in his MegaMonster mode, the Power Rangers must combine the Mega Mode power of their Zords to form the Samurai Megazord. But against a MegaMonster as strong as Robtish, even the Megazord isn't enough. The Rangers get an extra power boost from the Airstrike Combination, uniting the Samurai Battlewing and Samurai Megazord to create the Battlewing Megazord.

Battlewing Megazord

Kevin, the Blue Ranger, worked hard to devise a way to combine the aerial capabilities of the Samurai Battlewing with the fighting power of the Samurai Megazord. The result? The Battlewing Megazord. Piloted by the Red, Blue, Pink, Green, and Yellow Rangers together, the Battlewing Megazord takes the battle into the air.

INFO

Type	Megazord
Realm	Human world
Weapons	Megazord Katana
Skills	Flight
Special Attack	Flying Slash, Mega Spin Katana Strike

STATS
ADJUSTED FOR MEGA SIZE

INTELLIGENCE	10
STRENGTH	8
AGILITY	6
DAMAGE	8
CONTROL	8
COURAGE	10

ZORD SHOWDOWN

As an ordinary Nighlok Robtish was tough. It took the power of the Five Disc Tiger Cannon to defeat him. When he returns in MegaMonster mode, he's mega-tough. He wields his giant sword with deadly strength and skill. And to top it off, he can call in a flying Mooger air strike. If the Power Rangers want to defeat him, they'll have to work together to pilot their flying Megazord in some tricky aerial maneuvers.

Robtish

A deadly sword fighter with a Scottish accent, Robtish is so powerful that even the other Nighlok are afraid of him. His target is Jayden, the Red Ranger, who poses a special threat to Master Xandred. In his MegaMonster form, Robtish also commands a squadron of flying Moogers.

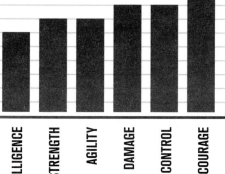

6 7 7 8 8 9	
INTELLIGENCE STRENGTH AGILITY DAMAGE CONTROL COURAGE	

STATS
ADJUSTED FOR MEGA SIZE

Nighlok MegaMonster	**Species**
Netherworld	**Realm**
Sword, Sonic Shock Wave	**Weapons**
Superb swordfighting ability	**Skills**
Double Slash	**Special Attack**

THE EXPERTS' PICKS

RED SAMURAI RANGER VS. DEKER
(PP. 8-9)
WINNER: DRAW

The opponents trade blow for blow. Neither can get inside the other's defenses. Jayden finally wounds Deker but is too exhausted to defeat him. With both fighters unable to continue, Deker withdraws.

PINK SAMURAI RANGER VS. DAYU
(PP. 10-11)
WINNER: PINK RANGER

Mia hesitates at first, but when Dayu unsheathes her dagger and attacks, the Pink Ranger's Samurai fighting reflexes take over. Faced with superior fencing, Dayu vanishes back to the Netherworld.

GREEN SAMURAI RANGER VS. ROFER
(PP. 12-13)
WINNER: ROFER

With giant fists pummeling from every direction, Rofer's Arm Stretch attack proves too much for the Green Ranger to handle on his own. Mike retreats.

BLUE AND PINK SAMURAI RANGERS VS. DOUBLETONE
(PP. 14-15)
WINNERS: BLUE AND PINK RANGERS

Together the Rangers parry the Nighlok's Tiger Tidal Wave. Simultaneous Dragon Splash and Airway attacks give Doubletone the double whammy, and he's down for the count.

SAMURAI BATTLEWING VS. DESPERAINO
(PP. 16-17)
WINNER: SAMURAI BATTLEWING

As expected, Desperaino takes the fight to the air. The Ranger pilots skim the Battlewing low to the ground, then fly up to release a Charging Slash. Desperaino goes down in flames.

GREEN SAMURAI RANGER VS. MOOGERS
(PP. 18-19)
WINNER: GREEN RANGER

The Mooger attacks with five of his cohorts, but it's no contest. Mike's Spin Sword weaves a slashing circle of steel. He takes out all six Moogers without breaking a sweat.

APEZORD VS. ANTBERRY
(PP. 20-21)
WINNER: ANTBERRY

Emily pilots the ApeZord in a ferocious charge, but her punches slip aside on Antberry's slime. Unable to try a dive from above without help from another flying Zord, the ApeZord leaves the fight.

YELLOW SAMURAI RANGER VS. NEGATRON
(PP. 22-23)
WINNER: YELLOW RANGER

Negatron lets fly with his insults and zingers, but Emily's immunity to his taunting make the Nighlok's chief weapon useless. The Yellow Ranger's Spin Sword takes him out of the picture.

GREEN AND BLUE SAMURAI RANGERS VS. SPITFANGS
(PP. 24-25)
WINNERS: GREEN AND BLUE RANGERS

The fireballs fly in a double Spitfang barrage. The Rangers split their opponents' fire by separating and attacking from opposite sides. The Forest Spear and Hydro Bow put the Spitfangs' fire out.

LIONZORD VS. TOOYA
(PP. 26-27)
WINNER: LIONZORD

The MegaMonster keeps the LionZord at bay with his double swords. But Jayden pilots the Zord in a Pentagonal Fury attack, hitting Tooya right between the eyes of his skirt-face.

BATTLEWING MEGAZORD VS. ROBTISH
(PP. 28-29)
WINNER: BATTLEWING MEGAZORD

Robtish's MegaMonster swordwork fails to penetrate the Megazord's defenses. From the cockpit, the Rangers counter with a Flying Slash, followed by a Mega Spin Katana Strike. Robtish is skewered.

POWER RANGERS SUPER SAMURAI

The Samurai Rangers' story continues as they meet new enemies and new allies. They unlock the secrets of more powerful Zords, and they find new ways to unite their powers as a team to battle the ever-growing evil plans of Master Xandred.

The key to unlocking the Rangers' new powers is an ancient talisman known as the Black Box. Retrieved from the Tengen Temple, Mentor Ji gave the ancient Black Box to Antonio, who worked hard to unlock it with his wizard-like programming skills. The Black Box gives Super Samurai powers to the Ranger who uses it. With the box, a single Samurai can call on the elemental Symbol Powers of all six Rangers: Jayden's power over fire, Kevin's water power, air for Mia, forest for Mike, earth for Emily, and light for Antonio. The box also lets a single Ranger pilot the Megazord combinations that would otherwise require all of the Rangers to control.

In the Netherworld, Master Xandred gains a new ally in the scissor-handed Nighlok Serrator. Serrator doesn't do his own fighting, instead sending lesser monsters and Papyrux robots to fight under his command. He also commands his own Nighlok minions, such as Maldan, who leads an army of laser blaster–wielding Master Blasters. Though he prefers to use others for his battles, Serrator can hold his own in a fight. Next to Master Xandred himself, Serrator is the most powerful Nighlok yet.

As the monster attacks increase in power, the Rangers gain new weapons, allies, and Zords. Antonio unlocks the power of the ancient LightZord, which serves both as a weapon and, in Mega Mode, as a giant humanoid fighter. Antonio also frees the power of the Shark Disc, giving them the powerful Shark Attack Mode and the SharkZord. A new ally, a boy named Cody, brings them the ancient BullZord, the first Zord ever created. Cody gives the Rangers another powerful weapon, the Bullzooka.

Meanwhile, old enemies appear on the scene. Serrator recruits Dayu as an ally, then she finds Deker, amazingly still alive after his duel with the Red Ranger. Because his sword, Urumasa, was broken in the original duel with Jayden, his curse has not ended. Serrator claims he can fix the sword, but only if Deker will help him with a secret plan to take over the world.

When he discovers Serrator's traitorous plan, Master Xandred appears in the human world and attacks both Serrator and the Samurai Rangers. Serrator escapes, and Jayden is badly injured. Before he can finish the Rangers off, Master Xandred dries out and must return to the Sanzu River to be rehydrated.

For the final part of his plan, Serrator returns Deker's sword and commands him to strike at a weakened spot in the earth, splitting the human world open and letting in the floodwaters of the Sanzu River. Sword in hand, Deker turns on Serrator. He won't do Serrator's bidding. All he wants is to fight the ultimate duel against Jayden. He leaves Serrator to face the Rangers, who defeat the scissor-fingered Nighlok in a furious battle.

With Master Xandred still recovering, Octoroo and Dayu escalate the battle by sending in the powerful monster Fiera. She uses the Red Ranger's own Fire Symbol Power and defeats him. He and the team are saved in the nick of time by the arrival of a new Secret Red Ranger, who turns out to be Jayden's older sister, Lauren. An old secret is revealed: it's Lauren, not her brother, who is trained in the power of the Sealing Symbol. Jayden leaves, turning the leadership of the group over to the new Red Ranger.

While the Rangers continue to battle the Nighlok invasions, Jayden goes off on his own. Deker finds him and challenges him to the truly final, ultimate duel. The two fight an epic battle, and Deker is defeated once and for all.

As the story nears its climax, Dayu, mourning the loss of Deker, releases all the sorrow stored in her harmonium. The Sanzu River pours into the human world and Master Xandred invades. In the course of the battle the Rangers are defeated and Lauren, injured and unable to continue, hands leadership back to Jayden. The Red Ranger leads the team back into the fight, for the final battle against Master Xandred.

BULL MEGAZORD VS. MALDAN

Declaring, "The era of the laser blaster is here!", the Nighlok Maldan marches into the human world at the head of an army of blaster-bearing Moogers. After defeating these Master Blasters and Maldan himself, it's time for the Power Rangers to face the giant Mega Maldan. For this contest, the Rangers will fight from the cockpit of the powerful Bull Megazord.

Bull Megazord

The ancient BullZord was the first Zord ever created. Mega Mode power transforms this already-gigantic Zord into the imposing Bull Megazord. In spite of its huge size, the Megazord is surprisingly quick and light on its feet. The Bull Megazord is armed with an array of shoulder-mounted blasters.

INFO

Type	Megazord
Realm	Human world
Weapons	Shoulder blasters, Mega Revolving Laser Blaster
Skills	Speed and agility
Special Attack	Raging Force

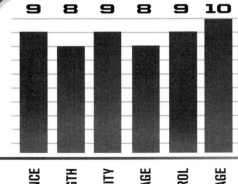

STATS
* ADJUSTED FOR MEGA SIZE

INTELLIGENCE	STRENGTH	AGILITY	DAMAGE	CONTROL	COURAGE
9	8	9	8	9	10

ZORD SHOWDOWN

Artillery is the key in this Mega Mode matchup. Maldan will call in the big guns, or one big gun, anyway: a huge laser blaster battle cannon that requires a crew of four giant Master Blasters. The Rangers will have to take out the Moogers and their cannon before the Bull Megazord can deal with Maldan himself. To match the Nighlok's heavy artillery, the Rangers will have to use the Megazord's Mega Revolving Laser Blaster.

Maldan

This Nighlok is more of a commander and tactician than close-in fighter. Maldan prefers have his brigade of Master Blasters do the fighting for him. But when his Mooger minions are defeated, Mega Maldan will pick up his own laser blaster and fire away with a devastating Barrage Attack.

		6	9	4	9	6	9

INTELLIGENCE · STRENGTH · AGILITY · DAMAGE · CONTROL · COURAGE

STATS
*ADJUSTED FOR MEGA SIZE

Nighlok MegaMonster	**Species**
Netherworld	**Realm**
Laser Blaster	**Weapons**
Laser blaster engineering	**Skills**
Barrage Attack	**Special Attack**

INFO

The Nighlok Armadeevil bounces into the human world like an armored ball of boastfulness, zapping people with laser beams and bragging that he's the greatest Nighlok ever to terrorize a human. In this matchup it's up to the Blue Power Ranger to serve him a double helping of humility. The contest won't be easy. Armadeevil's armor shell makes him nearly invincible.

Super Blue Ranger / Kevin

Using the Black Box, Kevin powers up to become the Super Blue Samurai Ranger. Super Samurai Mode is more than just a fancy jacket. It lets the Super Ranger call upon the Symbol Powers of all the other Rangers. With the Black Box attached, the Blue Ranger's weapon morphs into a Super Spin Sword.

INFO

Species	Human
Realm	Human world
Weapons	Super Spin Sword
Skills	Super Samurai kick
Special Attack	Super Spin Sword Slash

STATS

	INTELLIGENCE	STRENGTH	AGILITY	DAMAGE	CONTROL	COURAGE
	9	8	10	8	10	10

THE SHOWDOWN

The Blue Power Ranger's challenge will be to get inside Armadeevil's defenses. When the Nighlok curls up, his shell forms an unbroken sphere of plate armor. A Power Ranger's normal weapons aren't enough to crack this nut. To break through, Kevin will have to use the power of the legendary Black Box to morph into Super Samurai Mode. Only usable by one Power Ranger at a time, this battle mode gives the Ranger more powerful skills and weapons.

Armadeevil

This Nighlok's armor and main weapon are one and the same: an impervious, armadillo-like shell. Armadeevil curls up into a ball, then hurls himself at his enemies to knock them down like bowling pins. In his armored ball shape, it's nearly impossible for any weapon to touch him.

STATS

INTELLIGENCE	6
STRENGTH	8
AGILITY	8
DAMAGE	6
CONTROL	8
COURAGE	9

INFO

Species	Nighlok
Realm	Netherworld
Weapons	Invincible armor shell
Skills	Shoots laser beams from eyes
Special Attack	Rolling ball

37

TURTLEZORD VS. DUPLICATOR

When the Power Rangers fight the Nighlok Duplicator, their weapons pass through him as if he isn't there. That's because he isn't. The Rangers are fighting the mirror-image illusions that Duplicator uses to confuse his enemies. When he's finally defeated in spite of his trickery, he returns as a MegaMonster. In this match-up, the Pink Power Ranger faces the Mega Duplicator at the helm of the mighty TurtleZord.

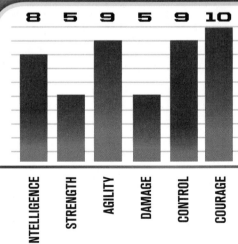

TurtleZord

The Pink Ranger transforms her Folding Zord into a giant flying Turtle with the power of the pink Turtle Disk. With Mia at the controls, the TurtleZord attacks by pulling in its head and flippers, then smashing into the enemy. When the Rangers' Zords combine into the Samurai Megazord, the TurtleZord forms the right arm.

INFO

Type	Zord
Realm	Human world
Weapons	Flying, spinning body
Skills	Flight
Special Attack	Aerial Turtle Strike

STATS
* ADJUSTED FOR MEGA SIZE

	8	5	9	5	9	10
	INTELLIGENCE	STRENGTH	AGILITY	DAMAGE	CONTROL	COURAGE

ZORD SHOWDOWN

Duplicator keeps his mirror-image ability even when he morphs to MegaMonster mode. The Pink Power Ranger's challenge will be to dispatch the mirror images first, then zoom in to attack the real Duplicator. By flying at top speed, the TurtleZord may be able to break through the crowd of copies fast enough to keep Duplicator from regenerating them. Then an Aerial Turtle Strike could finish him off.

Duplicator

This Nighlok has the power to create hundreds of mirror images of himself. Faced with an army of Duplicators, his opponents can't tell which one to attack. The real Duplicator taunts his enemies as they strike at the images that vanish into thin air.

STATS	
7	INTELLIGENCE
7	STRENGTH
6	AGILITY
7	DAMAGE
8	CONTROL
9	COURAGE

*ADJUSTED FOR MEGA SIZE

Nighlok MegaMonster	**Species**
Netherworld	**Realm**
Sword	**Weapons**
Can create mirror images of himself	**Skills**
Shoots purple energy blasts from hands	**Special Attack**

INFO

SHARKZORD VS. YAMIROR

In this matchup, the Samurai Power Rangers face off against the stinkiest Nighlok ever to seep through the cracks into the human world. Usually the Rangers would fight a MegaMonster Nighlok with the Samurai Megazord, but this time they'll have to keep their distance. As Yamiror tries to engulf the Megazord in a cloud of reeking breath, the Red Power Ranger sends in the SharkZord.

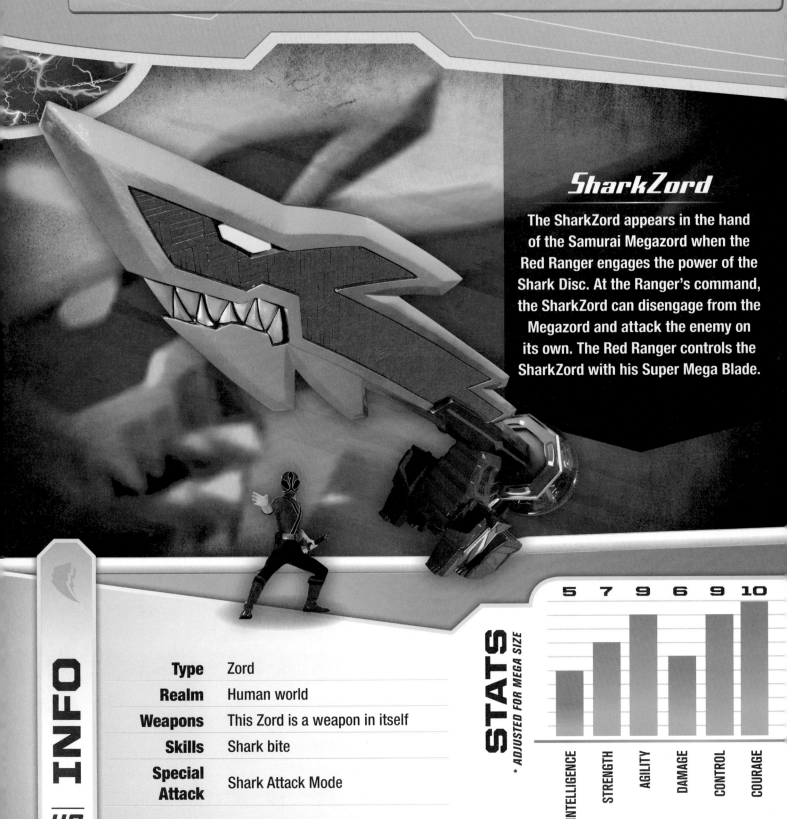

SharkZord

The SharkZord appears in the hand of the Samurai Megazord when the Red Ranger engages the power of the Shark Disc. At the Ranger's command, the SharkZord can disengage from the Megazord and attack the enemy on its own. The Red Ranger controls the SharkZord with his Super Mega Blade.

INFO

Type	Zord
Realm	Human world
Weapons	This Zord is a weapon in itself
Skills	Shark bite
Special Attack	Shark Attack Mode

STATS
*ADJUSTED FOR MEGA SIZE

INTELLIGENCE	STRENGTH	AGILITY	DAMAGE	CONTROL	COURAGE
5	7	9	6	9	10

ZORD SHOWDOWN

The Power Rangers will need to keep the Megazord far enough away from Yamiror to keep his toxic breath from filling the cockpit. The Red Ranger must first engage the Shark Disc to transform the Megazord into the Shark Megazord. Then he will disengage the SharkZord and send it in for the attack. Since there is no human aboard the SharkZord, it should be immune to Yamiror's evil breath. The matchup will come down to a contest between the MegaMonster's sword and the SharkZord's teeth.

Yamiror

Created when lightning struck a pile of toxic waste, this foul-smelling Nighlok can immobilize his enemies simply by breathing on them. Yamiror takes great pleasure in stinking up the environment, and he boasts about his vile stench. When the smell isn't enough to do the trick, he shoots bolts of energy from his eyes.

STATS
*ADJUSTED FOR MEGA SIZE

6	INTELLIGENCE
6	STRENGTH
5	AGILITY
5	DAMAGE
5	CONTROL
9	COURAGE

INFO

Nighlok MegaMonster	**Species**
Netherworld	**Realm**
StinkSword, Eye Blasters	**Weapons**
Can paralyze victims with his foul breath	**Skills**
Exhales stinking green mist	**Special Attack**

SECRET RED SAMURAI RANGER VS. FIERA

When Jayden, the Red Power Ranger, was put out of commission by a furious Nighlok attack, a mysterious Secret Red Ranger charged in to the rescue. The first heroic female Red Ranger ever, she turned out to be Jayden's older sister Lauren. Here, the Secret Ranger is matched against Fiera, a powerful Nighlok with special Red Ranger–targeting weapons.

Secret Red Ranger /Laruen

At a young age, Lauren was spirited away to master the Sealing Symbol her father used to trap Master Xandred in the Netherworld. She practiced her technique in hiding so she could focus solely on training, knowing she would return one day as the first female Red Samurai Ranger and true leader of the Samurai Power Rangers, fighting alongside her brother Jayden.

INFO

Species	Human
Realm	Human world
Weapons	Spin Sword, Fire Smasher, LionZord
Skills	Power over fire, mastery of the Sealing Symbol
Special Attack	Fire Smasher

STATS

9	6	8	7	9	10
INTELLIGENCE	STRENGTH	AGILITY	DAMAGE	CONTROL	COURAGE

THE SHOWDOWN

Fiera will try to use her Fire Flasher weapons to scorch Lauren from the inside out. The fearsome weapons, coupled with the MegaMonster Fiera's ability to fly from place to place almost instantly, mean that the Secret Red Ranger's only hope of defeating the Nighlok will be to attack at the controls of the LionZord. If Lauren uses the Zord to charge with an all-out blazing strike, she may have a chance for victory.

Fiera

This Nighlok was sent into the human world with one mission: to destroy Jayden, the original Red Samurai Ranger. With her Fire Flashers, Fiera harnesses the Symbol Power of the Red Ranger's own element, fire, to try to burn her enemy from within. She can flick from place to place with lightning speed.

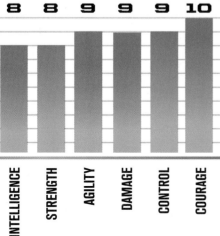

STATS

8	8	9	9	9	10
INTELLIGENCE	STRENGTH	AGILITY	DAMAGE	CONTROL	COURAGE

INFO

Nighlok	**Species**
Netherworld	**Realm**
Fire Flashers	**Weapons**
Super-fast flight	**Skills**
Can use the Red Ranger's own Fire Symbol Power	**Special Attack**

GOLD SAMURAI RANGER VS. OCTOROO

Master Xandred's sidekick Octoroo is the scholar of the Nighlok world. He spends much of his time poring over manuscripts to learn about the Power Rangers, discover new weapons, and devise schemes to further his master's evil plans. Here Octoroo is matched against Antonio, the Gold Power Ranger. A fisherman before he became a Power Ranger, Antonio is the ideal opponent for the squid-faced Nighlok.

Gold Ranger / Antonio

Antonio, the Gold Ranger, is a self-taught Samurai. A playmate of Jayden's when the two were kids, Antonio had to move away but swore to return as a Samurai Ranger. He is the tech wizard of the Power Rangers. The Gold Ranger's element is light. He commands the OctoZord and ClawZord.

INFO

Species	Human
Realm	Human world
Weapons	Barracuda Blade
Skills	Power over light
Special Attack	Barracuda Bite

STATS

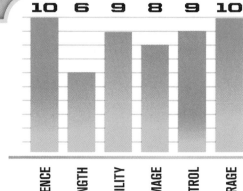

INTELLIGENCE	STRENGTH	AGILITY	DAMAGE	CONTROL	COURAGE
10	6	9	8	9	10

THE SHOWDOWN

Octoroo may seem comical, but he can hold his own in a fight. Both his staff and his eyes can fire powerful laser blasts. Whether he'll present a challenge to the Gold Power Ranger is another question. With his Barracuda Blade held in a backhand grip, Antonio is the fastest swordsman of the Power Rangers. On the other hand, Octoroo knows when to run away from a fight. Or, that is, make a strategic retreat.

Octoroo

Tentacle-faced Octoroo is Master Xandred's assistant aboard the Nighlok master's ship in the Netherworld. He has to put up with Master Xandred's foul moods, as well as nicknames like "Noodle-face," "Squid-lips," and "Sharkbait." Octoroo often travels to the human world to spy on the Power Rangers or check the progress of his plans and schemes.

45

STATS

9	5	6	5	7	5
INTELLIGENCE	STRENGTH	AGILITY	DAMAGE	CONTROL	COURAGE

INFO

Nighlok	**Species**
Netherworld	**Realm**
Staff	**Weapons**
Research and design	**Skills**
Laser blasts from eyes	**Special Attack**

DRAGONZORD VS. SKARF

The Nighlok Skarf eats his way through the city, gobbling up buildings, cars, and anything else that gets in his way. He has two mouths for twice the eating power, one at the end of each of his extendable arms. As a MegaMonster, Skarf has even more powerful weapons. The Blue Power Ranger, will face him at the controls of his DragonZord.

DragonZord

With Mega Mode power from the Blue Ranger's Dragon Disc, the DragonZord morphs from its six-sided Folding Zord form to an enormous blue dragon. Kevin pilots the Zord in airborne attacks on Nighlok MegaMonsters. When the Zords combine to make the Samurai Megazord, the DragonZord forms the left leg.

INFO

Type	Zord
Realm	Human world
Weapons	Fire breathing
Skills	Flight
Special Attack	Dragon Leap

STATS
*ADJUSTED FOR MEGA SIZE

INTELLIGENCE	STRENGTH	AGILITY	DAMAGE	CONTROL	COURAGE
8	6	9	6	9	10

ZORD SHOWDOWN

This voracious Nighlok's most formidable weapons only appear in MegaMonster mode. They're gigantic arms that fit together to form a full, body-length shield with built-in blasters. At the helm of the DragonZord, the Blue Power Ranger's best strategy will be to zoom in close and wait for Mega Skarf to take a swing at the Zord with his fists. When Skarf's arms separate for the punch, a blast of DragonZord flame may just get inside his defenses.

Skarf

With a pair of devouring mouths at the ends of his arms, this Nighlok literally eats everything in sight. Skarf can extend his arms over long distances to gobble up objects or fight Power Rangers. But his real power, a gigantic shield, doesn't appear until his MegaMonster phase.

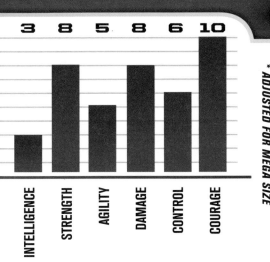

STATS
ADJUSTED FOR MEGA SIZE

3	8	5	8	6	10
INTELLIGENCE	STRENGTH	AGILITY	DAMAGE	CONTROL	COURAGE

Nighlok MegaMonster	**Species**
Netherworld	**Realm**
Mouths on arms, giant shield with blasters	**Weapons**
Eating, eating, and more eating	**Skills**
Arms stretch for long-distance eating	**Special Attack**

INFO

47

CLAW BATTLEZORD VS. PAPYRUX

Tech wiz Antonio, the Gold Power Ranger, has programmed his lobster-shaped ClawZord to morph into the mighty Claw Battlezord. The versatile Battlezord can take different forms, each with different weapons. In this matchup, the Claw Battlezord takes on Papyrux, a robot snipped out of paper by the powerful Nighlok Serrator. He may be paper, but the Mega-sized Papyrux is anything but a lightweight.

Claw Battlezord

The Mega Mode ClawZord morphs into the Claw Battlezord for mega-attack. The Battlezord has four different forms: North, South, East, and West, chosen by spinning a control disc in the cockpit. The Claw Battlezord North wields the OctoZord as a weapon in spear form.

INFO

Type	Zord combination
Realm	Human world
Weapons	Claws, swords, Octo Spear
Skills	Can morph into four different forms
Special Attack	Claw Pincer Slash, Octo Spear Charge

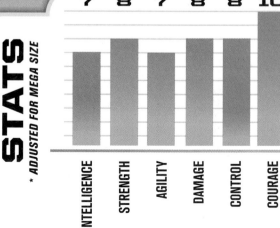

STATS
*ADJUSTED FOR MEGA SIZE

INTELLIGENCE	STRENGTH	AGILITY	DAMAGE	CONTROL	COURAGE
7	8	7	8	8	10

ZORD SHOWDOWN

Papyrux's strength is his expert swordsmanship. At the controls of the Claw Battlezord, the Gold Power Ranger will have to choose the mode that will be best for defense, yet has the power and weaponry to take down the robot. Against a fencer like Papyrux the best bet may be the Claw Battlezord South, which wields a pair of swords. Or Antonio could go for the changeup, switching from form to form in the middle of the fight.

Papyrux

This Nighlok robot grows to Mega size from a paper cutout. He obeys his master Serrator's every command. A lightning-fast fencer, Papyrux fights with a double-bladed sword that resembles a pair of deadly scissors. He can also throw a flaming ball of energy at his opponents.

9	6	6	7	7	5
INTELLIGENCE	STRENGTH	AGILITY	DAMAGE	CONTROL	COURAGE

STATS
*ADJUSTED FOR MEGA SIZE

Nighlok MegaMonster	**Species**
Netherworld	**Realm**
Double-bladed sword	**Weapons**
Superb fencer	**Skills**
Energy blast	**Special Attack**

INFO

BEARZORD VS. SWITCHBEAST

The devious Switchbeast has a snarling, wolf-like face in the middle of his chest. This Nighlok uses his spirit-switching power to trap his victims' spirits inside discarded pieces of junk. Luckily, the Power Rangers are able to force him to return the spirits to their owners' bodies before the objects are destroyed. Once vanquished, the Switchbeast returns as a MegaMonster. Here he faces the Green Power Ranger's BearZord.

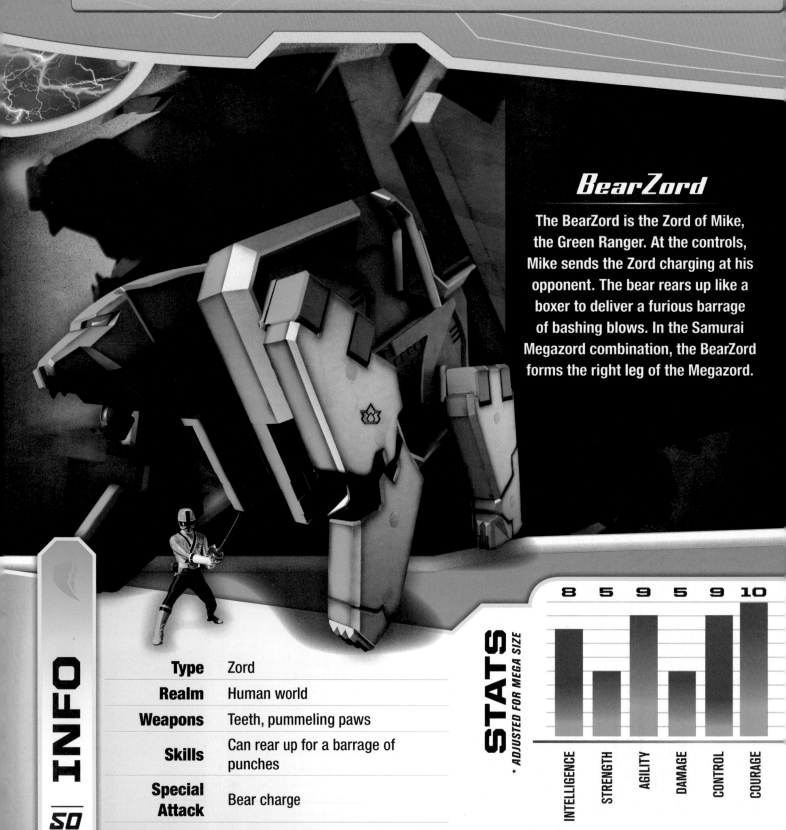

BearZord

The BearZord is the Zord of Mike, the Green Ranger. At the controls, Mike sends the Zord charging at his opponent. The bear rears up like a boxer to deliver a furious barrage of bashing blows. In the Samurai Megazord combination, the BearZord forms the right leg of the Megazord.

INFO

Type	Zord
Realm	Human world
Weapons	Teeth, pummeling paws
Skills	Can rear up for a barrage of punches
Special Attack	Bear charge

STATS
ADJUSTED FOR MEGA SIZE

8	5	9	5	9	10
INTELLIGENCE	STRENGTH	AGILITY	DAMAGE	CONTROL	COURAGE

ZORD SHOWDOWN

The Switchbeast's most dangerous attack is the Switch Blast. If he can trap his opponent's spirit in an inanimate object, the fight will be over. Luckily, the Green Power Ranger is protected inside the BearZord, where the Switchbeast's switching tentacles can't touch him. Instead, the Nighlok will attack with his double-headed spear and Switch Blast fireballs. With the determined power of the BearZord, the Green Ranger has very good odds in this matchup.

Switchbeast

The Switchbeast has the power to trap humans' spirits in inanimate objects, leaving the people's bodies frozen in place like statues. In MegaMonster mode, this Nighlok fights with a double-headed spear. In the special Switch Blast attack mode, he spews fireballs from his wolf-like mouth.

STATS
*ADJUSTED FOR MEGA SIZE

INTELLIGENCE	STRENGTH	AGILITY	DAMAGE	CONTROL	COURAGE
7	8	6	7	6	9

INFO

Nighlok MegaMonster	**Species**
Netherworld	**Realm**
Spear-tipped switching tentacles, double-headed spear, fireballs	**Weapons**
Traps humans' spirits in inanimate objects	**Skills**
Switch Blast	**Special Attack**

CLAW ARMOR MEGAZORD VS. GRINOTAUR

When humans are sprayed with toxic dirt by the Nighlok Grinotaur, they develop a case of the killer munchies. The victims eat and drink without stopping until they make themselves sick, then they eat even more. The munchies go away when Grinotaur is defeated, but, as always happens, the Nighlok returns as a MegaMonster. Here the Power Rangers challenge Mega Grinotaur at the controls of the Claw Armor Megazord.

Claw Armor Megazord

Using the Black Box with the Samurai Combination Disc, the Power Rangers can combine the Samurai Megazord with the Claw Battlezord to create the colossal Claw Armor Megazord. With all of their Symbol Powers united by the Black Box, the entire Power Ranger Samurai team pilots this Megazord.

INFO

Type	Megazord
Realm	Human world
Weapons	Sword pair
Skills	Uses the united Symbol Powers of all six Rangers
Special Attack	Double Katana Strike

STATS
* ADJUSTED FOR MEGA SIZE

INTELLIGENCE	STRENGTH	AGILITY	DAMAGE	CONTROL	COURAGE
10	9	6	9	8	10

ZORD SHOWDOWN

The opponents in this matchup have two different fighting styles. Grinotaur prefers to throw exploding pods from a distance. The Claw Armor Megazord is best at close-in fighting with its pair of short katana swords. If the Power Rangers can pilot the Megazord to dodge the exploding pods, they should be able to do well against Grinotaur. But they'll have to beware of the Nighlok's explosive killer head-butt attack.

Grinotaur

Grinotaur spews toxic, hunger-inducing dirt from his aardvark-like snout. This Nighlok's body is covered with gourd-shaped pods. When fighting, he detaches them from his body and flings them at his enemies like exploding dodgeballs. For an extra attack, he can shoot a barrage of blue energy bolts from his forehead.

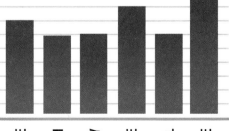

7	INTELLIGENCE
6	STRENGTH
6	AGILITY
8	DAMAGE
6	CONTROL
9	COURAGE

STATS
* ADJUSTED FOR MEGA SIZE

INFO

Nighlok MegaMonster	**Species**
Netherworld	**Realm**
Sword, exploding pods, blue energy bolts	**Weapons**
Spits toxic dirt that causes insatiable hunger and thirst	**Skills**
Killer head-butt	**Special Attack**

53

LIGHT MEGAZORD VS. EPOXAR

For centuries, Samurai tried without success to unlock the power of the ancient LightZord. It took a lot of hard work, but Antonio, the Gold Power Ranger, finally managed to release its Symbol Power and wield the LightZord against the Nighlok. In Mega Mode, the LightZord becomes the agile Light Megazord. In this contest the Megazord takes on Epoxar, a Nighlok who shoots globs of glue.

Light Megazord

Programmed by Antonio, the lantern-like LightZord expands with Mega Mode power into a towering martial arts expert. The Gold Ranger controls the Light Megazord with text-message commands from his Samurai Morpher. The Megazord can also blind his opponents with a blaze of light or pummel them with a barrage of Battle Discs.

INFO

Type	Megazord
Realm	Human world
Weapons	Hands, feet, Battle Discs, blazing light power
Skills	Martial arts mastery
Special Attack	Battle Disc Scattershot, Mega Spin Attack

STATS
*ADJUSTED FOR MEGA SIZE

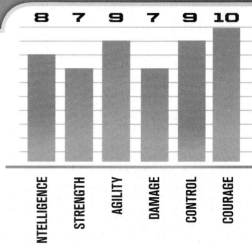

INTELLIGENCE	8
STRENGTH	7
AGILITY	9
DAMAGE	7
CONTROL	9
COURAGE	10

ZORD SHOWDOWN

Things could get sticky in this contest. The extra mouth on Epoxar's shoulder spits out blasts of glue that can immobilize his opponent. This MegaMonster also wields a battle fork with four scythe-like blades. The Light Megazord's advantage in this contest is his speed and agility. If he can dodge the blobs of glue, he may be able to take Epoxar down with a Battle Disc Scattershot or Mega Spin Attack.

Epoxar

This Nighlok's victims really stick together. The glue from Epoxar's glue shooter hardens into an unbreakable bond that won't let go until he is defeated in battle. In one particularly devious attack, he spreads a layer of glue on the ground to trap any Power Ranger that steps on it.

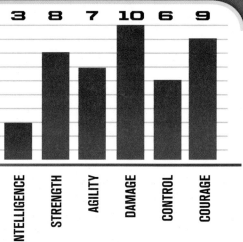

3	8	7	10	6	9
INTELLIGENCE	STRENGTH	AGILITY	DAMAGE	CONTROL	COURAGE

STATS
* ADJUSTED FOR MEGA SIZE

Species	Nighlok MegaMonster
Realm	Netherworld
Weapons	Glue spewer, laser blasts, battle fork
Skills	Can stick his opponents together or immobilize them with globs of glue
Special Attack	Glue trap

SAMURAI SHARK MEGAZORD VS. RHINOSNORUS

The snooze-inducing Rhinosnorus blows out a mist that sends his human victims to sleep. Then the Nighlok enters their dreams to try to eat the dreamers. If eaten in the dreamworld, the victims never wake up in the real world. In this matchup, Rhinosnorus faces off in MegaMonster mode against the Power Rangers in the Samurai Shark Megazord. The Megazord combines the powers of the Samurai Megazord and the SharkZord.

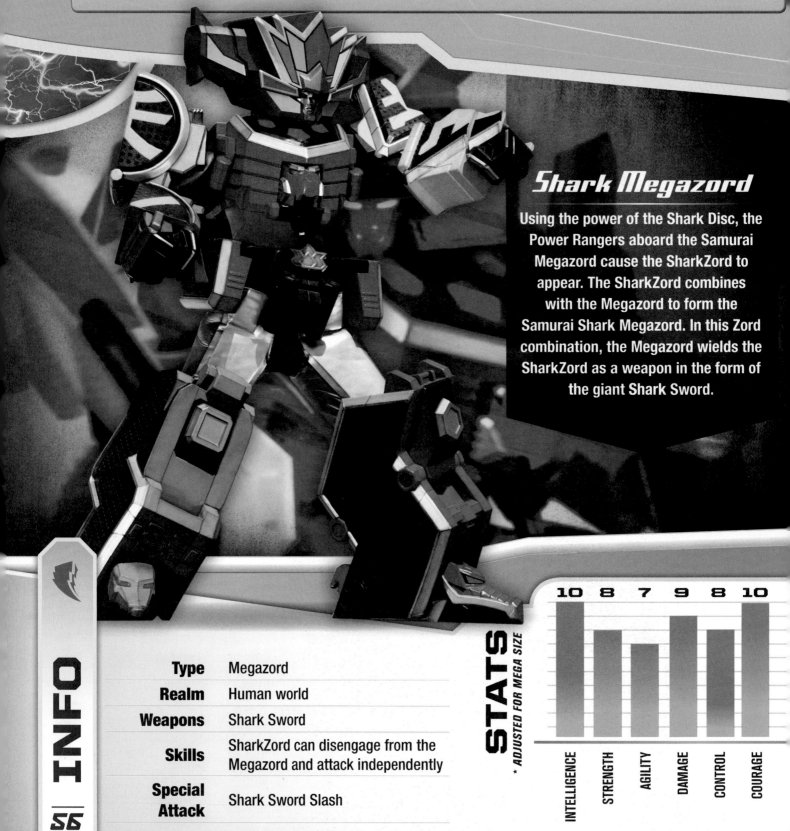

Shark Megazord

Using the power of the Shark Disc, the Power Rangers aboard the Samurai Megazord cause the SharkZord to appear. The SharkZord combines with the Megazord to form the Samurai Shark Megazord. In this Zord combination, the Megazord wields the SharkZord as a weapon in the form of the giant Shark Sword.

INFO

Type	Megazord
Realm	Human world
Weapons	Shark Sword
Skills	SharkZord can disengage from the Megazord and attack independently
Special Attack	Shark Sword Slash

STATS
ADJUSTED FOR MEGA SIZE

10	8	7	9	8	10
INTELLIGENCE	STRENGTH	AGILITY	DAMAGE	CONTROL	COURAGE

The key for the Power Ranger team will be to cut off Rhinosnorus's mist blower. With the blower out of commission, he can't send his opponents to sleep, and his already-sleeping victims will awaken. For his part, Rhinosnorus will use his special hopping, stomping attack to shake up the Megazord and rattle the nerves of the Rangers in the cockpit. If the Rangers can hold their concentration, a Shark Sword Slash from the Megazord should end the contest.

Rhinosnorus

Rhinosnorus's mist blower puts out a cloud of sleep-inducing fog. This nightmarish Nighlok wants his victims to have a pleasant time in their dreams, so they'll be all the more delicious when he enters the dreamworld to eat them. The "sleeping snacks" can only be woken by defeating Rhinosnorus.

STATS
*ADJUSTED FOR MEGA SIZE

8	6	9	6	7	9
INTELLIGENCE	STRENGTH	AGILITY	DAMAGE	CONTROL	COURAGE

INFO

Nighlok MegaMonster	**Species**
Netherworld	**Realm**
Sword, sleep mist blower	**Weapons**
Can enter people's dreams	**Skills**
Earth-shaking hop attack	**Special Attack**

57

CLAW ARMOR MEGAZORD AND SAMURAI BATTLECANNON VS. DREADHEAD

The Power Rangers use the power of the Black Box to combine the Samurai Battlewing, itself a combination of three animal Zords, with the OctoZord to create the Samurai BattleCannon. The BattleCannon won't work by itself. The Rangers must work as a team to fire the cannon from the cockpit of the Claw Armor Megazord. Here, they call out the big guns against the Nightlok MegaMonster Dreadhead.

Claw Armor Megazord and Samurai BattleCannon

This double Megazord combination uses nearly every animal Zord under the Power Rangers' command. The Lion, Turtle, Ape, Bear, Dragon, and Claw Zords combine to form the Claw Armor Megazord. Then the Tiger, Beetle, Swordfish, and Octo Zords combine to create the BattleCannon. The cannon becomes the Megazord's Mega-weapon.

INFO

Type	Zord combination
Realm	Human world
Weapons	The BattleCannon is the weapon
Skills	Unleashes the power of all of the animal Zords together
Special Attack	BattleCannon Blast

STATS
ADJUSTED FOR MEGA SIZE

INTELLIGENCE	STRENGTH	AGILITY	DAMAGE	CONTROL	COURAGE
10	10	5	10	7	10

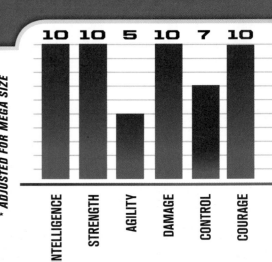

ZORD SHOWDOWN

Dreadhead is tough to damage because most weapons pass right through his body. Even the Samurai Megazord's katana sword can't touch him. But with the addition of the BattleCannon, the Claw Armor Megazord becomes one of the most powerful Megazords ever. A BattleCannon blast should make short work of the dreadlocked Nighlok, but the Power Rangers will have to aim carefully. The BattleCannon uses so much Symbol Power that it can only be fired once during the fight.

Dreadhead

This Nighlok can waver between dimensions so that weapons pass right through his body without causing harm. Dreadhead only breaks off a battle is when his body starts to dry up from spending too long in the human world. Then he must return to the Sanzu River to rehydrate.

7	6	10	5	8	9
INTELLIGENCE	STRENGTH	AGILITY	DAMAGE	CONTROL	COURAGE

STATS
* ADJUSTED FOR MEGA SIZE

Nighlok MegaMonster	**Species**
Netherworld	**Realm**
Sawed-off blaster	**Weapons**
Good at making bad puns	**Skills**
Weapons can't touch him	**Special Attack**

INFO

59

CLAW BATTLEZORD NORTH AND BULL MEGAZORD VS. SERRATOR

In this matchup, it takes a pair of powerful Megazords to face the MegaMonster Serrator. With Master Xandred confined to his ship in the Netherworld, Serrator is the most powerful Nighlok ever to cross over into the human world. Though he claims to be doing the Master Xandred's bidding, Serrator has secret plans of his own, and they don't include his supposed boss.

Claw Battlezord North and Bull Megazord

This Megazord team actually features three Zords: the Claw Battlezord North is a combination of the Claw Megazord and the OctoZord. The Claw Battlezord is controlled by the Gold Ranger, while the Red Ranger pilots the Bull Megazord. Together, the two Megazords sport a fearsome array of weaponry.

INFO

Type	Zord combination
Realm	Human world
Weapons	Mega Octo Spear, shoulder blasters, Mega Revolving Laser Blaster
Skills	Speed, agility, martial arts mastery
Special Attack	Octo Spear Charge, Raging Force

STATS
*ADJUSTED FOR MEGA SIZE

INTELLIGENCE	STRENGTH	AGILITY	DAMAGE	CONTROL	COURAGE
10	9	8	9	8	10

ZORD SHOWDOWN

In spite of their arsenal of skills and weaponry, it's going to take superb coordination and massive power for this Megazord team to stand up to the MegaMonster Serrator. If the past is any indication, the Nighlok will call on the help of a giant Papyrux robot and a pair of Spitfangs. The Red and Gold Power Rangers will first have to defeat Serrator's minions before going after the MegaMonster himself. The outcome is far from a sure thing.

Serrator

Scissor-handed Serrator is the second most powerful Nighlok after Master Xandred. He prefers to hatch evil plans and have others do the fighting for him, but Serrator himself is a nearly invincible fighter. His secret plan is to get rid of Master Xandred and rule both the human world and Netherworld.

STATS *ADJUSTED FOR MEGA SIZE		
INTELLIGENCE	9	
STRENGTH	9	
AGILITY	9	
DAMAGE	9	
CONTROL	9	
COURAGE	10	

Nighlok MegaMonster	**Species**
Netherworld	**Realm**
Extendable scissor-like claws, soccer-style energy ball	**Weapons**
Can create Mega-sized Papyrux robot by cutting it out of paper	**Skills**
Energy-blasting soccer kick	**Special Attack**

INFO

SAMURAI GIGAZORD VS. MASTER XANDRED

The ultimate matchup pits the Samurai Gigazord against Master Xandred, Lord of the Netherworld. The Gigazord is the most powerful Zord combination, uniting the power of all ten of the Power Rangers' animal Zords. Master Xandred is the most powerful Nighlok of all, with a burning hatred of the Power Rangers and a desire to flood the human world with the waters of the evil Sanzu River.

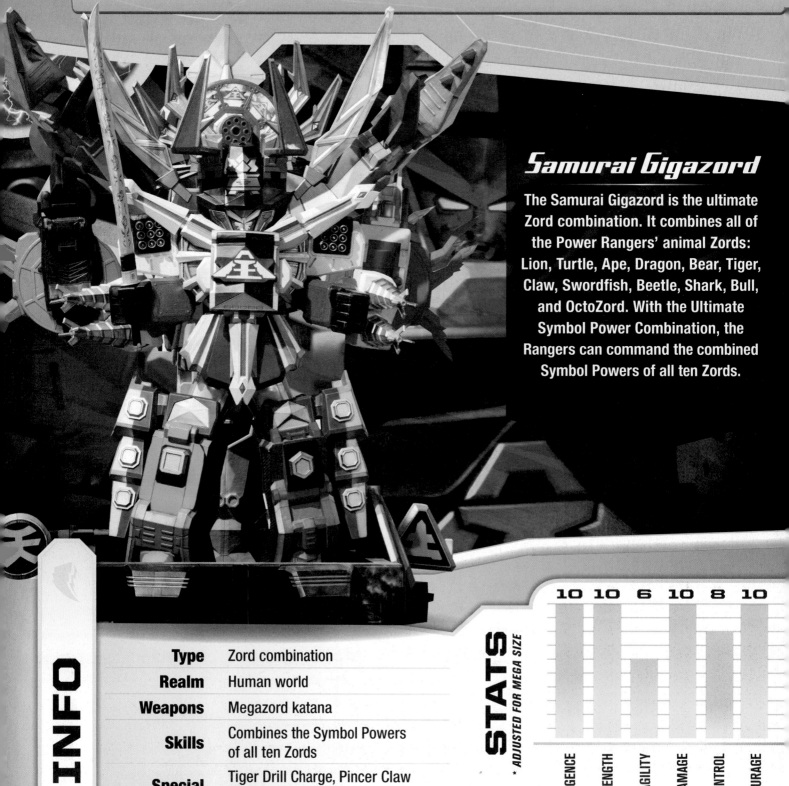

Samurai Gigazord

The Samurai Gigazord is the ultimate Zord combination. It combines all of the Power Rangers' animal Zords: Lion, Turtle, Ape, Dragon, Bear, Tiger, Claw, Swordfish, Beetle, Shark, Bull, and OctoZord. With the Ultimate Symbol Power Combination, the Rangers can command the combined Symbol Powers of all ten Zords.

INFO

Type	Zord combination
Realm	Human world
Weapons	Megazord katana
Skills	Combines the Symbol Powers of all ten Zords
Special Attack	Tiger Drill Charge, Pincer Claw Attack, Ultimate Samurai Slash, Symbol Power Mega Strike

STATS
*ADJUSTED FOR MEGA SIZE

10	10	6	10	8	10
INTELLIGENCE	STRENGTH	AGILITY	DAMAGE	CONTROL	COURAGE

ZORD SHOWDOWN

The battle will likely come down to a Mega-sized fencing match, the opponents facing off with their huge katana swords. At the helm of the Samurai Gigazord, it will take every ounce of the Power Rangers' skill and Symbol Power to match Master Xandred. But they'll have a fighting chance. As six skilled Samurai working together, the Rangers have the advantage of teamwork. And Master Xandred can only spend a limited amount of time away from the Sanzu River before drying up.

Master Xandred

Imprisoned for years aboard his ship at the bottom of the Netherworld's Sanzu River, Master Xandred found a way to break the seal and resurface. Since that time, he has been sowing misery among humans in order to flood the world by swelling the Sanzu waters with human tears.

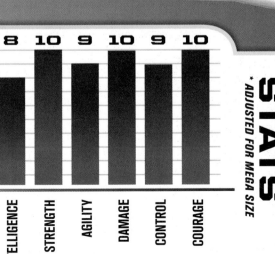

8	10	9	10	9	10
INTELLIGENCE	STRENGTH	AGILITY	DAMAGE	CONTROL	COURAGE

STATS
* ADJUSTED FOR MEGA SIZE

Nighlok MegaMonster	**Species**
Netherworld	**Realm**
Evil katana	**Weapons**
Flight	**Skills**
Darkness spell	**Special Attack**

INFO

THE EXPERTS' PICKS

BULL MEGAZORD VS. MALDAN
(pp. 34–35)
WINNER: BULL MEGAZORD

Maldan blasts away with a Barrage Attack, but he's no match for the superior speed and agility of the Bull Megazord. The Rangers take him down with a counter-barrage from the Megazord's shoulder blasters.

SUPER BLUE SAMURAI RANGER VS. ARMADEEVIL
(pp. 36–37)
WINNER: ARMADEEVIL

As expected, Armadeevil curls into an impenetrable ball. Even in Super Samurai mode, Kevin can't crack his armor. The Blue Ranger retreats after Armadeevil bounces on him.

TURTLEZORD VS. DUPLICATOR
(pp. 38–39)
WINNER: DUPLICATOR

Mia flies the TurtleZord in charge after charge, but Duplicator's reflections multiply faster than she can dispatch them. She and the Zord break off the fight to go for help.

SHARKZORD VS. YAMIROR
(pp. 40–41)
WINNER: YAMIROR

The Rangers keep their distance and send the SharkZord to attack. The Zord gnaws on Yamiror's legs but doesn't do enough damage. The Rangers call the Zord back and regroup for a different strategy.

SECRET RED SAMURAI RANGER VS. FIERA
(pp. 42–43)
WINNER: SECRET RED RANGER

It's a close fight, but Lauren uses her Samuraizer to call on the Mega Mode power of the LionZord. A last-ditch Blazing Strike followed by the Zord's flaming Furious Lion Howl, and Fiera is toast.

GOLD SAMURAI RANGER VS. OCTOROO
(pp. 44–45)
WINNER: GOLD RANGER

As predicted, the Gold Ranger's Barracuda Blade is too fast for Octoroo to handle. The squid-headed Nighlok runs away to fight another day.

DRAGONZORD VS. SKARF
(pp. 46–47)
WINNER: SKARF

Skarf's tiki-faced shield proves to be impenetrable by one Zord alone, even in Mega Mode. Unable to damage the giant Nighlok, Kevin flies the DragonZord back to get reinforcements.

CLAW BATTLEZORD VS. PAPYRUX
(pp. 48–49)
WINNER: CLAW BATTLEZORD

Antonio tries a first attack with the Claw Battlezord South, but Papyrux parries the Battlezord's blades. Calling on the extra power of the OctoZord, the Gold Ranger defeats the paper robot with the Claw Battlezord North.

BEARZORD VS. SWITCHBEAST
(pp. 50–51)
WINNER: BEARZORD

Unable to call on his spirit-switching power, the Switchbeast is forced to fight with his other weapons. Mike takes the BearZord in a lumbering charge and pummels the Switchbeast to the ground.

CLAW ARMOR MEGAZORD VS. GRINOTAUR
(pp. 52–53)
WINNER: GRINOTAUR

In a surprising upset, Grinotaur keeps the Megazord at a distance with a barrage of grenade-like pods. Then an explosive head-butt attack knocks the Megazord down. The Rangers back the Megazord off.

LIGHT MEGAZORD VS. EPOXAR
(pp. 54–55)
WINNER: EPOXAR

Epoxar proves a tough opponent for the Megazord. Antonio blinds the Nighlok with a blaze of light, then fires a Battle Disc Scattershot attack from the Megazord, but Epoxar responds wth a blast of glue seizing up the Megazord and forcing retreat.

SAMURAI SHARK MEGAZORD VS. RHINOSNORUS
(pp. 56–57)
WINNER: SAMURAI SHARK MEGAZORD

The Megazord's Shark Sword makes short work of Rhinosnorus's mist blower. The Nighlok's hopping attack doesn't rattle the Rangers' resolve, and the Megazord defeats him with a Shark Sword Slash.

CLAW ARMOR MEGAZORD AND SAMURAI BATTLECANNON VS. DREADHEAD
(pp. 58–59)
WINNER: MEGAZORD TEAM

The Nighlok can dodge a sword, but he's no match for the combined power of all the Zords together. A single, carefully aimed BattleCannon blast hits Dreadhead dead-on, and the battle is over.

CLAW BATTLEZORD NORTH AND BULL MEGAZORD VS. SERRATOR
(pp. 60–61)
WINNER: MEGAZORD TEAM

Serrator sends in his Papyrux-and-Spitfang advance team. The Rangers' Megazord duo defeats them after a hard fight. Alone and faced with two opponents, Serrator escapes back to the Netherworld.

SAMURAI GIGAZORD VS. MASTER XANDRED
(pp. 62–63)
WINNER: TOO CLOSE TO CALL

The Samurai Gigazord is the Rangers' ultimate fighting vehicle, but Master Xandred is the ultimate Nighlok. The opponents are too closely matched for the experts to call a winner.